Well, Let Me Just Tell Y'all

Chris W. Scholl

WESTBOW
PRESS®
A DIVISION OF THOMAS NELSON
& ZONDERVAN

Scripture quotations marked NASB are taken from the New American Standard Bible, Copyright 1960, 1962, 1963, 1968, 1971, 1972, 1973, 1975, 1977, 1995 byThe Lockman Foundation. Used by permission.

Scripture quotations marked TLB are taken from The Living Bible copyright 1971. Used by permission of Tyndale House Publishers, Inc., Carol Stream, Illinois 60188. All rights reserved.

Cover design by Brant and Brittnye Schroeder
Brenda Osbourne - photographs of Solar Powered
Light, Dandelion, Red Leaf poem
Susan Sudduth – Painting for Bradford Pear Poem
Lindsey Guercio, Moon and Stars and Boy With Red Balloon
Other photos by author

WestBow Press books may be ordered through booksellers or by contacting:

WestBow Press
A Division of Thomas Nelson & Zondervan
1663 Liberty Drive
Bloomington, IN 47403
www.westbowpress.com
1 (866) 928-1240

ISBN: 978-1-5127-5923-5 (sc)
ISBN: 978-1-5127-5924-2 (hc)
ISBN: 978-1-5127-5922-8 (e)

Library of Congress Control Number: 2016916602

Print information available on the last page.

WestBow Press rev. date: 12/14/2016

Contents

Introduction

In early 2012, I reached a point in my spiritual life that I never thought I would face. Allow me to explain. In 2010, my husband and I had separated because of an incredibly difficult marriage. At the age of 40, due to complications from diabetes, he had his first heart attack and was diagnosed with kidney failure. This led to his need for kidney dialysis three times a week. Because of the decline in his health, it became evident that he could not live alone anymore, so he moved back home. About a year after that, he contracted an infection in his leg which required him to have it amputated from the knee down. During all of this, we owned a business that I loved doing and took great pride in. But, it had come to a point that I had to decide between a business that required so much of me and an ailing husband. I chose to sell the business and started working part-time while running a smaller version of the business on the side. Many, many other things led up to this difficult time in our lives, but selling the business was the final straw for me.

I had been a good kid growing up, I rarely got into trouble and tried very hard to lead a Christian life. I grew up in a loving home and church; I had a close relationship with God which I carried into my adult life. I had prayed fervently for my husband's health. I had asked God for children, but we were not able to have any. I had prayed for my business, seeking guidance and growth. I had given our marriage to Him so many times, and we continued to struggle. Why would a loving God let all this happen to me?

What was I doing wrong? Where was He? Why bother with this prayer thing? So, I stopped. I gave up. God wasn't listening to me so why should I pursue this relationship any longer?

However, God did not let me off that easy. He never gave up on me. He continued to pursue me. This time of separation from God lasted only a few months, before I slowly began to crawl back to Him. He began to show me His love through little, every day things. Through those little things, I started searching through His Word and writing these things down. The relationship between me and my husband began to change. Despite my efforts to guard my heart, we grew closer than we had ever been. Yes, we still had struggles, but the outlook was different. A year later, I signed up to join my church on a mission trip to Kenya.

My husband and I were not really in a place financially to send me on such an incredible trip. Therefore, if God wanted me there, He was going to have to provide the funds. So, for the next six months, I worked to raise the money for this trip. During that six months, legal issues arose involving the sale of my business, my dogs got into a bad fight that resulted in a veterinarian bill of over $2,500, and there were issues over the arrangements for medical care for my husband while I was gone. Satan attempted to keep me away, but he failed. Through the generosity of friends and family, God not only provided the funds for the trip, but He also provided the money to fly my husband to his sister's who cared for him while I was away. The Lord saw to it that we both had spending money, my loss of income was covered, and the costs of our pets' care was taken care of. Not only that, the legal issues were resolved (not necessarily the way I had hoped, but it did not affect me financially), the medical arrangements finally lined out, and through the generosity of an anonymous person and my veterinarian, that veterinarian bill was paid IN FULL! The mission trip was amazing, but the journey to get there was the *real* reason God wanted me to go. I could tell so many stories of the incredible blessings I received during that time.

I returned from that mission trip in early August, 2013. Just four months later, my husband passed away.

If God had let me go when I wanted to leave Him, if He had not continued to pursue me, if I had not seen His mighty works through those months of fund-raising, if God had answered my prayers the way I wanted them answered, I would not have been able to handle what was to come that December and the years that have followed.

My husband loved to worship. So instead of a traditional funeral service, we had a *worship* service. My church's praise team led the music and I worshipped as I would have if it had been a regular Sunday morning, because that is what my husband would have wanted. During that service, three words were repeated over and over again...those three words were GOD IS GOOD.

No matter what life throws our way, no matter what WE think we need, no matter how WE think a prayer should be answered, GOD IS GOOD.

God has continued to teach me BIG lessons through LITTLE things and I have continued to search His Word for what He is wanting me to learn. And ya know what? There is always a verse to go along with what I feel God is teaching me that day. God's Word was written by men that lived over two thousand years ago, and it is still true today. He is so GOOD.

In truth, some days are just better than others, but God continues to renew my strength daily with the lessons He teaches me. I would love to share how my Heavenly Father cares for me, and I hope that it will inspire you to search for ways in which He will show His love to you.

So, join me for a moment and, *let me just tell y'all!*

Thank You!

Thank you Mom and Dad! Your support is beyond comprehension. I am so blessed to have such Godly parents that have taught me and shown me the love of Christ.
Thank you Paula Bledsoe for believing in me and encouraging me to reconnect with my creative side.
Thank you Freedom Church family (my fellow Freedomites) for *Doing Love* [1], for showing me how to worship, for your heart for missions, for strengthening me and for your endless inspiration.

Photograph and Artwork Acknowledgements

Brenda Osbourne, photographer and friend extraordinaire!
Brenda provided photography for *Red Leaf, Dandelion*, and *Solar Light*.
For more of her wonderful photography, visit facebook.com/indigo-wild-photography

Lindsey Guercio, just a Junior in High School, with an incredible heart!
Lindsey provided the sketches for *Moon and Stars* and *Boy with Red Balloon*.

Sharon Sudduth, a friend I hold dear to my heart.
Sharon provided the beautiful painting for *Bradford Pear in Spring*.
To see more of Sharon's work, visit Etsy.com.
Her shop is called SharonSudduthStudio.

In *Memory* of:
Patrick Scholl and his incredible parents,
Edward and Billie Jean Scholl
Dorothy Tabb, maternal Grandmother
Will Watson, paternal Grandfather (AKA Papa)

O Lord God, Thou
has begun to show
Thy servant Thy greatness
and Thy strong hand;
for what god is there in heaven
or on earth who can do such works
and mighty acts as Thine?

-Deuteronomy 3:24

Re-*P*URPOSED Pieces

My grandmother was a china painter - and a talented one at that. When my husband and I got married, her gift to us was a full set of dishes that she had painted pink roses on. The collection included full place settings, large serving pieces, salt and pepper shakers, and a butter dish. There are so many pieces in the collection, that I cannot display them all. Therefore, I have several pieces on display in my china cabinet, and many are carefully tucked away behind the lower cabinet doors. That china cabinet happens to have belonged to my grandmother. I inherited it when she passed away.

Several years ago, my parents were visiting for Thanksgiving, so I used the china my grandmother had painted. After our dinner, my mom and I were washing the dishes, and as we were putting them away, one of the plates fell to the floor and broke into several pieces. The shattered plate broke my mom's heart, as it was her mother who had painted the beautiful pieces.

The plate was beyond repair. Instead of throwing the pieces away, I put them in a bag and stored them safely in a drawer. I held on to those pieces for several years until I decided to do something with them for my mom for Mother's Day. I took the broken pieces and created a mosaic cross. Now, the plate has purpose again.

We all start our lives as a beautiful plate. God created us with a unique design for a purpose. He painted us with our own look, personality, passions, gifts, talents, strengths and even our weaknesses.

When we break, He is there to pick up the pieces and Re-Purpose us so we can continue on the path that He created us for. When God *repurposes* us, He *re*-directs us and *re*-stores us for the *purpose* He designed us for; *re-purposing.* Whether you are facing something now, have already been through something, or are about to endure something that breaks you, God has a plan for you and will take the brokenness and *re*-create the piece that He intended for you to be. He never intended for us to be broken and tucked away for no one to see.

The broken plate was out of sight, and in a plastic bag for several years, just waiting for the right time to be used again. God's timing is perfect. He has a plan and will see to it that we are ready to carry out our part when the time comes.

Truly I have spoken; truly I will bring it to pass. I have planned it, surely I will do it.

- Isaiah 46:11b

$\mathcal{D}$own Spout

One year, I decided it was time to have my roof replaced. Springtime in Oklahoma usually means lots of storms, so I thought I better have the roof done before the crazy weather began. The roofers came, and in three days, they removed the old roof and replaced it with the new just in time for the spring showers to arrive. One day during a little rain shower, I happened to notice my gutters were not working properly. Upon inspection, I discovered the roofers had not cleaned all of their debris out of the gutters, so it had collected at the bend in the downspout where the rain flows out into the yard. The junk had clogged my downspout so the water could not flow.

Not long after that, as I was trying to wrap things up for this book, I had something happen that really upset me. In all honesty, I was flat-out angry about the situation. As I struggled with it, God reminded me of the clogged downspout. When we allow junk to build up, we block the flow of God's work through our lives. If we want to be a part of what God is doing, it is important to keep the channels open so God's purpose can flow efficiently to the world around us.

The junk that clogs our downspouts is not necessarily always bad. For instance, there is a section of my guttering, under the overhang of my roof, that is about a foot long; it connects the gutter from the roof to the downspout. Every year, a bird builds a nest there. The bird's nest is a good, beautiful thing. I enjoy watching the birds and following that whole process of nature as it develops, but it does hinder the flow of rain through my gutter system. Similarly, we can get caught up in doing all the things we think are good or right and before we know it, we get overloaded and overwhelmed. Soon, the good stuff collects in our downspouts and blocks the flow of what God intends for us.

We are downspouts - vessels for God. He has a purpose in mind for us. When we let the gunk of this world clog our minds, we hinder the flow of His will for our lives.

Watch over your heart with all diligence,

For from it flow the springs of life.

- Proverbs 4:23

Who among all these does not know that the hand of the Lord has done this, in whose hand is the life of every living thing, and the breath of all Mankind?

- Job 12:9-10

Solar Power by SON-light

There are many uses for solar-powered lights: landscaping, wedding décor, and DIY projects, just to name a few. My dad likes to "piddle" with solar lights. There is a corner of my parent's yard that lights up like the Parade of Lights at Disney World when the sun goes down. It is really kind of fun.

The way solar-powered lights work is that they absorb the sunlight during the day, and then when the sun goes down, the lights come on using that stored-up power from the sun.

As Christians, we have a constant source of light. If we absorb the light God provides for us, we can find the power to shine when darkness sets in.

There is no doubt we are going to face darkness. But, if we soak up the SON-light by worshipping, spending time in prayer, reading His word, fellowshipping with believers, seeking Godly counsel, counting our blessings, or simply finding joy in the little things, we can shine through the darkness - not only for ourselves, but for those around us.

I have come as light into the world, that everyone who believes in Me may not remain in darkness.

\- John 12:46

Got Things to Do

I have had a pet-sitting business for many years. One of my clients is an elderly gentleman who lives in a retirement community. He has a cool Scottish terrier named Lewis that I walk several times a day. Our first walk of the day is usually between six thirty and seven in the morning. When the weather is nice, there is a spunky ole lady who lives down the street from my client who gets her walker on wheels out and walks around the block a few times. We usually walk past each other and exchange "Good Mornings," and then carry on. One particular morning as we walked by each other, she commented on how dark it was starting to get and then she said something that kind of made me chuckle. She said, "I usually don't like to get up this early, but I've got things to do!" Here she was living in a retirement center, probably in her late seventies or early eighties, and *"she's got things to do!"*

Paul tells us in 1 Corinthians 15:58 to be "steadfast, immovable, *always abounding in the work of the Lord,* knowing your toil is not in vain in the Lord" (my emphasis). Many characters of the Bible - beginning with Abraham, Moses, and David, and on to Paul, James, and John - were known to be *abounding in the work of the Lord* well into their dying days. In fact, many of them were killed because of their work for the Lord.

Jesus Himself was always busy. In John 5:17, He tells us that His "Father is always at work to this very day, and that I, Myself am working."

Whether we can run or need a walker to get around, or whether we are young and healthy or facing our last days, we are to be about our Father's business.

We have *got things to do!*

Whatever you do, do your work heartily, as for the Lord rather than for men;

- Colossians 3:23

This I recall to my mind,
Therefore I have hope.
The Lord's lovingkindnesses indeed never cease,
For His compassions never fail.
They are new every morning;
Great is Thy faithfulness.
"The Lord is my portion," says my soul,
"Therefore I have hope in Him."

- Lamentations 3:21-24

Boy with the *R*ed Balloon

Garage sales are a big part of summer. From October to April, garage sales are sort of "out of season" because of the cold and unpredictable weather. One year, a friend of mine decided to bring the garage-sale experience inside. She gathered a few friends who pulled their things together and dragged it all to our local community center for an indoor garage sale. I participated in this event. The room was bustling with chatter and laughter as the thrifty shoppers rummaged from booth to booth. Suddenly, there was an outburst of tears. Everyone turned around to see a young boy standing in the middle of the room, holding a red balloon and bundled up in his winter coat. For some unknown reason, he was just standing there crying his little heart out.

The scene was funny, yet sweet and heartbreaking at the same time. But what a great depiction of how we often react to the blessings and miracles of God. Instead of seeing the joy in our red balloon (our blessings), we are all too often overcome by the world and what we do not have. We stand in the middle of everything throwing our little tantrum, and we fail to see the insurmountable blessings around us.

The Bible teaches us over and over again to remember what God has done for us. Yet remembering is not easy. Life throws so many hardships our way that we tend to let go of our red balloon and grasp the negativity that surrounds us.

Nevertheless, God is so good that He brings new mercies every day. He knows we will forget, so He reminds us over and over and over and...over.

Thank you Lord that you remind us daily of your mercy, power, blessings, strength, and love.

Weathering the Storms

I love animals, I always have. I can't remember a time that I did not have a pet of some sort; if there was, it was not for very long. At any rate, as of today, I have 5 dogs and 4 cats and am fostering a dog for a local rescue organization. As one could imagine, this many animals in one house can present many challenges. However, they also make me laugh on a daily basis, they have comforted me through many difficult times in my life, and they have taught me so many life lessons. One of those lessons occurred a few years ago when a bad storm rolled through town.

On this particular night, I actually had 7 dogs in my house and 4 cats. Five of the dogs were my own, and I had just rescued 2 others. This storm had blown in with high winds, heavy rains, and loud claps of thunder and brilliant flashes of lightening. Each of my dogs reacted to the storm differently. Hannah, my old beagle, was frantic for a bit but was heard snoring under my bed within minutes. She had found solace in what she considered a safe place. Kramer, my sweet shepherd mix laid on the bed as close to me as he could get. He would tremble when the thunder roared across the night sky. Duffy, my other goofy shepherd mix, paced and breathed heavily for a bit, but finally got comfortable on the dog bed that laid next to mine. Oscar, an old yellow Labrador that I had just rescued anticipated the storm hours before it arrived. Once it reached us, he simply could not be calmed down. He jumped on the bed, he jumped off the bed, he walked to the front of the house, he ran to the back of the house, and whined the entire time. He did not rest until the storm had passed. Pippin was the other Labrador mix that I had just rescued. She laid at the foot of the bed with her ears perked up, alert and ready to fight whatever the storm might bring. Tatum, my Great Dane mix, and Mary, my other old beagle laid in their favorite sleeping spots, sound asleep with no care in the world.

How do you react when a storm hits?

Storms are in our forecast. They are going to come and go. Some storms may be more intense than others, some may cause damage and some may just bring a nice cooling rain. No matter how hard we try to avoid them, we are going to face them. You may react like Hannah and find comfort in a safe place. Maybe you are like Kramer and fear certain aspects of the storm. The storm may make you nervous at first until you realize you are going to be okay. You may be like Oscar and anticipate the bad weather before it hits. Then you are nervous from then until the storm passes. Maybe the changes in the weather heighten your awareness of what is around you and you stand guard, ready to face whatever may come. Or, just maybe, you are able to weather the storm with the peace of knowing everything is going to be okay in the end.

Yes, storms are in our forecast. You may be experiencing partly cloudy skies, or bright shining days. The skies may be overcast, or you may be smack-dab in the center of a raging hurricane. God is in the midst of any weather life brings our way. He may calm the storm or He may be there with an umbrella, walking beside us protecting us from the rains that fall. No matter how we react to the weather, God is there to see us through it. We can rest in knowing that much is true.

Do not be afraid, O Zion;
Do not let your hands fall limp.
The Lord your God is in your midst,
A victorious warrior.
He will exult over you with joy,
He will be quiet in His love,
He will rejoice over you with shouts of joy.

- Zephaniah 3:16-17

And they became very much afraid
and said to one another,
"Who then is this,
that even the wind and the sea obey Him?"

-Mark 4:41

15

God thunders
with His voice
wondrously,
Doing great
things which
we cannot
comprehend.
For to the snow
He says, "Fall
on the earth,"
And to the
downpour and the
rain, "Be strong."
He seals the
hand of
every man.

That all men may
know His work.

-Job 37:5-7

Evening Sky

Not that I am biased or anything, but my niece is incredibly smart. One day, my dad, who she calls Papa, was teaching her how to draw stars. I actually remember him teaching me how to draw stars when I was a little girl. My dad is one of those hands-on grandfathers. He comes by that naturally because his dad, who was my Papa was the same way.

Anyway, he drew a few stars and the moon on a piece of paper and asked my niece what that was. He was expecting her to describe the shapes, such as "that's a star and that's a moon" as any 5-6-year-old would do. Instead, her response was, "that's the *evening sky*."

My wise niece's comment reminded me of the limited vision we have of our lives and what is happening in the world around us. The sun, moon, and stars we gaze upon are just small flickers of light compared to the full expanse of the heavens. Our human-ness restricts our ability to see it all. Yet, God's vision has no boundaries.

Imagine your life – your past experiences and the life you are living right now – as the sun, moon and stars. That is all you can see, but God can see the *evening sky*. That same God created you, He has a plan for you, He loves you, and He is in control.

When I consider Thy heavens,

the work of Thy fingers,

The moon and the stars,

which Thou has ordained;

What is man, that Thou

dost take thought of him?

And the son of man, that

Thou dost care for him?

- Psalm 8:3-4

The Moon and Stars

When night falls, the moon and stars come out to play.
The Moon stands tall; the stars take their place.
They have a role that they've performed for years
To bring light to a world as darkness draws near.

These lights of darkness never fail to shine.
They always perform their parts; they know their lines.
When the sun goes down, the Moon takes the lead
The stars join in for all the world to see.

Clouds often come to block the view of their play,
But they carry on, they perform anyway.
They sing, they dance, they tell a great story
Of a God who reigns with almighty glory.

Like the Moon and stars that always take the stage,
Our Heavenly Father is there, forever and always.
We may not see Him because of life's clouds,
But He never leaves, this He has vowed.

So enjoy the performance, take in each scene,
As another day closes, the actors begin their routine.
Remember the promise their story tells
Of a God who loves us and never fails.

Thou alone are the Lord.
Thou hast made the heavens,
the heaven of heavens with all their hosts,
The earth and all that is on it,
The seas and all this in them,
Thou dost give life to all of them
And the heavenly host bows down before Thee.

- Nehemiah 9:6

30% *Heart*

My husband had diabetes, which led to heart and kidney disease. As if that was not enough, he also suffered from a condition called Essential Tremors. This condition caused his hands to tremor, or shake. The intensity of the tremors made many everyday activities difficult for him. A few months before he passed away, he was looking forward to undergoing a procedure called Deep Brain Stimulation which would minimize, if not stop, the debilitating tremors. Before he could have the procedure, doctors had to make sure his heart was strong enough, so they ran several tests. The results of the tests showed my husband's heart was working at 30%.

The day after we got the results, I was driving to work and thinking about what that meant for my husband's health. Then, I heard God asked me this question, "What percentage of *your* heart is working?" I knew He didn't mean my physical heart. Ouch.

God calls us to LOVE Him will all of our heart (Deuteronomy 6:5[2]). We are to SERVE Him with a whole heart (1 Chronicles 28:9[3]) and He wants our full devotion (1 Kings 8:61[4]). Our WHOLE HEART, that means 100%, not 25%, 60%, 75% or even 99%.

No, WHOLE means WHOLE.

The condition of a person's heart is rarely visible to the naked eye. Doctors use instruments and technology to diagnose the health of the heart. Oftentimes, the spiritual condition of the heart is not easily seen either, but nothing is hidden from God. He searches the heart (1 Chronicles 28:9 and Jeremiah 17:10[5]), He looks at the heart (1 Samuel 16:7[6]), and He knows the secrets of the heart (Psalms 44:21[7].)

As with the human heart, there are ways we can improve the condition of our spiritual heart. Through exercises such as Bible Study, prayer, worship (my favorite), and Christian fellowship, we can grow closer and closer to that 100% mark. And, just as making the physical heart stronger is not always easy, exercises and lifestyle for spiritual health is not easy either.

No matter where your heart is now, you can just call on God to help you develop a more spiritually fit heart. God wants our whole heart.

...know the God of your father, and serve Him with a whole heart and a willing mind; for the Lord searches all hearts and understands the intent of the thoughts.
- 1 Chronicles 28:9

FREEDOM

"Aye, fight and you may die. Run, and you'll live... at least a while. And dying in your beds, many years from now, would you be willin' to trade ALL the days, from this day to that, for one chance, just one chance, to come back here and tell our enemies that they may take our lives, but they'll never take... OUR FREEDOM!" ~ William Wallace, *Braveheart*

Once you accept Jesus as your savior, you are given freedom that cannot be taken away. There is an enemy who is ruthless, clever, and evil who will stop at nothing to attempt to take that freedom away. There will be days you feel hopeless. You will have days that it seems the price of living for Christ costs too much. You will face trials, sicknesses, failures, and doubts. And the enemy will use all of that to his advantage. However, no matter how hard the enemy tries, his attempts are futile because of what Jesus did for you on the cross.

God sent His Son so we could have freedom. The enemy threatens to rob us of our joy, steal our peace, and defile our innocence. He will use any weapon possible to take our lives, but he cannot and will never be able to take...OUR FREEDOM.

*Now the Lord is the Spirit;
and where the Spirit of the
Lord is, there is liberty.*

- 2 Corinthians 3:17

*It was for freedom that Christ set us
free; therefore keep standing firm and do
not be subject again to a yoke of slavery.*

- Galatians 5:1

Change the Battery

Why do we press harder on a remote control when we know the batteries are getting weak?

That was a question a friend posted on social media a while back. It's a good question is it not?

Why DO we press harder? I do not know about any of you, but not only do I press the buttons harder, but I push them repeatedly and wave the remote around as if trying to find a signal. Sometimes I even tap the remote on something as if I can tap just a little more juice out of the batteries. Why do I do all that when all I have to do is recharge or change the batteries?

As a follower of Christ, our Source of Power never gets weak, but our connection to that power often does. We get so caught up in life and lose our charge that our strength is depleted and our system shuts down. Instead of plugging in to the source of power God has for us, we push harder or repeatedly which often gets us nowhere or we find ourselves just worn out.

We do not have to rely on our own power as we face what life throws our way. God is all powerful and the power He offers is readily available to all who choose to "plug-in" to His resources.

...that your faith should not
rest on the wisdom of men, but
on the power of God.

- 1 Corinthians 2:5

But we have this treasure in
earthen vessels, that the surpassing
greatness of the power may be of
God and not from ourselves;

- 2 Corinthians 4:7

$\mathcal{W}$hiteboard of Forgiveness

Every Easter, as many churches do, my church holds a Good Friday service. One year, our pastor asked us to come to the front where he had set up a few large white boards. He asked us all to write a sin, or as many sins as we wanted to on that board. When I went forward to participate in the assignment, I glanced at what others had already written on the board. There were words like greed, pride, jealousy, faithlessness, anger, and so forth. In the midst of all these words, a child had written, "Hitting my brother".

What a sweet reminder of our God's forgiveness. God sent His Son as a sacrifice for our sins, no matter how small or large they are. That sweet child recognized that he/she had done something wrong and wanted to be forgiven for it. And guess what! God forgave him/her because He loves and honors those who seek forgiveness.

There was a time when hitting my little brother might have been the only sin I knew about that day, because I got in trouble for it. Quite frankly, I doubt that I asked forgiveness for my actions. However, God reminded me on that particular Good Friday that He forgives me for that past sin, and He forgives me now as I write words like anger, doubt, struggles to love and forgive my enemies, complaining, and bitterness.

He forgives *every* sin.

After we had all had a chance to write something on the board, our pastor painted over all the words on the boards with red paint. That is what Good Friday is about isn't it? God sent His Only Son to die a brutal death so that through the power of the blood that was shed, we could be forgiven.

I acknowledged my sin to Thee,

And my iniquity I did not hide;

I said, "I will confess my transgressions

to the Lord"; and Thou didst

forgive the guilt of my sin.

- Psalm 32:5

...knowing that you were not redeemed with

perishable things like silver or gold from

your futile way of life inherited from your

forefathers, but with precious blood, as of a lamb

unblemished and spotless, the blood of Christ.

- 1 Peter 1:18-19

Hey, Batter Batter!

"Hey, Batter Batter!"

Whether you attend a Little League Game, a Minor League Baseball Game, or the Major Leagues, you hear, or you have been the one yelling, "Hey, Batter Batter!" to the player who is standing in the batter's box waiting for the pitcher to throw him the ball. A good baseball player trains himself to focus on the pitcher. The batter should be so in tune with the pitcher and keeping his eye on the ball, that nothing else around him matters until he swings that bat.

In life, there are voices in the stands that are yelling at us, trying to distract us from the ball and the Pitcher. Those voices are getting louder and more distracting, so it is getting harder and harder to stay focused. If we want to keep our focus on what is right, we must train harder and practice more to learn how to tune out the fans from the opposing team.

Just like the baseball player, if we start to listen to the voices around us or lose focus on the Pitcher, we may swing at something that is not a good pitch, we might get hit by the ball, or we might just stand there and watch the ball fly by us and miss the opportunity to get on base or even hit a home run.

The Pitcher stands on the mound - ready to throw the ball. Are you focused on Him and ready to swing at the ball, or are the noises in the stands distracting you?

Let your eyes look directly ahead,
And let your gaze be fixed straight in front
of you. Watch the path of your feet,
And all your ways will be established.

- Proverbs 4:25-26

...fixing your eyes on Jesus, the author
and perfecter of faith, who for the joy set
before Him endured the cross, despising
the shame, and has sat down at the
right hand of the throne of God.

- Hebrews 12:2

"He is not here, but He has risen. Remember how He spoke to you while He was still in Galilee, saying that the Son of Man must be delivered into the hands of sinful men, and be crucified, and the third day rise again." And they remember His words.

- Luke 24:6-8

As *He* Said

Jesus awoke. He opened His eyes but could not see anything because of the cloth that covered His face. Bloody linens bound His body. He could smell the fragrance of the myrrh and aloe that He could also feel tucked between His fingers.

Jesus drew in as deep a breath as the linens would allow and as He exhaled, He spoke, "Father."

The earth began to shake. Through the shroud that covered His face, He could see the brightness that shown around Him and could feel the warmth of its brilliance. Through the quake, He heard a powerful, yet loving voice, "My Son." The linens that bound His body began to loosen and the shroud fell off His face as if blown off by a gentle breeze.

Jesus sat up, then rose to His pierced feet. The quake settled and the glorious light faded. Now, the light from the morning sun filled the darkness of the tomb, and Jesus walked toward the entrance. As He stepped out into the sunlight, His eyes focused. To the right of Him, there were two men who were trying to regain their composure from the shock of the quake and unexplainable light. Jesus recognized the men. They were Roman Soldiers that had been a part of His crucifixion just days before. He turned to examine the scene behind Him and saw the opening to the tomb where His crucified body was lain to rest. The massive stone that was meant to secure the tomb was resting to the left of the opening, and large chunks of rock were scattered on the ground around it.

Jesus looked above the tomb and saw two more men. They were built much like the Roman soldiers, but there was something supernatural – no divine about them. He recognized these men as well, they were part of His Father's army; the angels who had been given the awesome task of bringing His Son home. The men smiled and waved for Jesus to come. Jesus climbed the rock to join the men, and they embraced each other as brothers would that had not seen each other in years.

Jesus turned to take one final look at the scene around Him, then He and the Angels walked into a light that seemed to engulf them before it disappeared.

Another chunk of rock fell to the ground and landed at the feet of the two Soldiers who were left in awe of what had just happened.

He has Risen Indeed.

Grandpa Watson's Chair

My dad inherited his great-grandfather's rocking chair.
One summer, he decided to restore the old chair. When
my dad works on something like this, he does not just
dive in and get to work, he studies what he is working
on and makes plans before getting to the actual labor.
We jokingly say he is doing some "figurin" before
he starts working on something. He takes special
measures to make sure every detail is just right.

The first step to restoring the old chair was to take the
chair apart. That had to be done carefully because of
the age of the chair. Then, he stripped away the paint
that had been a part of the chair for many years. One
of the rockers had broken, so my dad had to repair
that. He did some research, and then constructed
a new one. Next, my dad repainted the wood and
carefully put all the pieces back together, securing
each piece. Finally, the back and seat of the old chair
were completely worn and tattered and needed to be
replaced. The back and seat are the most important
parts of a chair. They must, not only be comfortable,
but durable enough to withstand a fair amount of
weight. Without the back and seat, the chair is not
fulfilling the purpose for which it was created. My
dad kept this in mind as he studied various types of
twine to use and ways to weave that twine. Once he
chose the right materials, he and my mom took on the
tedious task of weaving the seat and back by hand.
Now - the chair could be used again, and for years to
come.

Grandpa Watson's chair is a beautiful reminder of what God does for us. When we are worn out, completely broken, and tattered, or when we feel like we are scrap for the wood pile, or too old to be of use anymore, God desires to restore us to even better condition than we were before. He scrapes away the old paint, mends the broken pieces, adds a new coat of paint, fits the parts back together, and lovingly secures the finished product. Then, He restores an important aspect of His creation - our heart. Our bodies may be structurally sound, but if our heart is worn and tattered, we may not be strong enough to fulfill the purpose for which we were designed. So, before God puts us back to work, He weaves our hearts back together with His strength, love, forgiveness, endurance, power, and grace.

God has a purpose for us and intends to see us through to the completion of that purpose. Sometimes, it just takes the hand of craftsman to keep us going.

*For if these qualities are yours
and are increasing, they render
you neither useless nor unfruitful
in the true knowledge of our
Lord Jesus Christ.*

- 2 Peter 1:8

For we are His workmanship,
created in Christ Jesus
for good works, which God
prepared beforehand, so that
we should walk in them.

- Ephesians 2:10

Stunted Growth

I have had one of those typical, basic house plants
in my kitchen window for years. I have repotted it,
taken broken pieces and started new plants, and cut
back dead growth to keep the silly thing around. A
few years ago, a small sprout broke off, so I put it in
a terrarium that I had purchased for my husband
when he was in the hospital. Although the plants that
came with the terrarium had died, I could not bring
myself to throw the container away, after all, the other
elements of the terrarium were still alive. I carefully
placed the sprout in the dirt and rocks and place the
lid on top. Terrariums are easy to care for. All they
require is a little water every now and again and
nature takes care of the rest. If anything, it would be
interesting to see what would happen.

The little sprout has grown to fill the terrarium. The
roots are healthy, and the little plant seems quite
happy in the little glass jar. The leaves are pretty, but
they are quite smaller than the leaves of the "mother"
plant. Sure, the little sprout grew and seems quite
content where it is, but by putting it in a small glass
jar, I kept it from being as big or full, as it could have
been. I stunted its growth and kept it from its full
potential.

How often do we do that to ourselves? We either see
ourselves as incapable of doing something, or we
do not think we can attain something because of a
weakness, lack of ability, or whatever. We allow the
words of others, or something that has happened in

the past to thwart what we are truly capable of doing now or in the future. More than that, we do not trust that God will give us what we need to fulfill something He has called us to do. There are so many thoughts, emotions, and fears that weigh us down, that much like the little sprout, we confine ourselves to our little glass container where we are safe and quite comfortable. We keep the lid on our terrarium and simply *survive*.

Not long after I planted that little sprout in the terrarium, I cut off another piece of the plant and simply placed it in a vase with water in it. That growth is now about four feet long and hangs down from the top of my china cabinet. The leaves are actually *larger* than the "mother" plant, and the roots are plentiful.

That is what God wants for us. If we remove the lid to our glass container and trust in His power, His word, His omniscience, His love, His strength - whatever He needs to give us to *thrive* like the larger plant, He will give it to us. All we have to do is open our eyes, ears, hearts and souls to what He is calling us to do and to believe He will see us through it.

And he will be like a tree firmly
planted by streams of
water, which yields its
fruit in its season, and its
leaf does not wither;
and in whatever he does, he prospers.

- Psalm 1:3

The *B*radford Pear *B*looms in Spring

The Bradford Pear Tree blooms in Spring.
Winter is over, its blossoms sing.
The white petals, so full and thick.
Like white cotton candy on a stick.

Spring brings storms of wind and rain
And scatters the petals, and blows them away.
They cover the streets, fields and roof tops,
Painting the world with little polka dots.

The Bradford Pear blooms in Spring.
A sign of Hope, and a peace offering.
When the petals blow here and there,
That hope, to the world those blossoms share.

What if those that follow Christ
Were like those blossoms when storms arise?
We'd cover the streets, fields and roof tops,
With a love and hope that never stops.

Our Source of Hope is always there
For us to cling to and for us to share.
Storms will come and winds will blow.
That is the time for us to GO.

For us to share the Hope everlasting
To those that need His peace offering.
He loves us all so much He died.
And even more, that Hope is alive.

The Bradford Pear blooms in Spring.
A loving song of hope everlasting.
The storms will come and winds will blow.
A time to share so the world will know.

*W*ater Stations

I have never run a marathon. In fact, the only time I run any distance is when I am chasing a dog that has gotten away from me. However, I have *walked* in a few charitable events. In either situation, it is common for there to be water stations strategically set up along the path of the walk or race. Volunteers are posted at the stations to cheer the participants on and to hand them a cup or bottle of water to drink.

Jesus offered us Living Water so we would never thirst again. Those who accept the water He gives, live with a promise of an eternal life with Him and His Father. It is true that we will never thirst again, but I believe God has strategically placed points along the paths of our lives that are like those drink stations of a race.

For me, those stations may include friends who call, text, or send a card, a smile from a child who is sitting in the buggy in front of me at the grocery store, a ladybug landing on my shoulder, reading a scripture I have never seen before, watching birds and squirrels frolic in the trees of my front yard, visiting with my neighbor, attending Sunday worship, hearing particular songs on the radio, finding a dollar on the ground, an afternoon nap, the daily laughter my animals provide, or making my elderly customers laugh. It is through those little things that make me smile that I find refreshment and strength to continue on to the next leg of the race.

The point is, God does not just give us the water He promised, and then leave us to fend for ourselves through the rest of the race. He knows we are going to face disappointment, failure, doubt, discouragement and fear, so He Himself will be at the next station, or He will appoint someone to meet us there to see us through.

You may be that "someone" God has called to stand post at a station as a runner passes by. You may be asked to give someone guidance, wisdom, forgiveness, love or just a word of encouragement. You may even be asked to run alongside someone to help him/her through to the next leg of the race or as they cross the finish line. We are all running this marathon. We will all face times in our lives when we are tired, scared, weary, or in need.

God meets us along the course of the race to give us what we need to keep going. We are not running the race alone.

Yet those who wait for the Lord
will gain new strength; They will
mount up with wings like eagles,
They will run and not get tired,
They will walk and not become weary.

Each one helps his neighbor,
and says to his brother,
"Be Strong!"

- Isaiah 40:31, 41:6

...so *Christ* also, having been offered once to bear the sins of many, shall appear a second time for salvation without reference to sin, to those who eagerly await *Him*.

- *Hebrews* 9:28

Be dressed in readiness, and keep your lamps alight.
And be like men who are waiting for their master when he returns from the wedding feast, so that they may immediately open the door to him when he comes and knocks.

- *Luke* 12:35-36

Wait for it...wait for It!

In the beginning...God has always been and will always be. He has time in His hands.

Before He created the world, I imagine God encompassing the atmosphere and saying to the planets, "Wait for it...wait for it." Then, by simply speaking, He threw all the planets, stars, moon and sun into orbit. He created earth and all of existence began.

Old Testament stories tell of the sinful nature of God's people and their need for a savior. Many of them hear Him speak and trust His promises. To them, He said, "Wait for it...wait for it." Then, He worked in miraculous and wondrous ways to insure His promises would be kept.

Then, centuries passed where God's people believe He was silent, but I imagine Him preparing the heavens and telling them to "Wait for it...wait for it...wait for it." Then, He fulfilled His promise through the birth of His Only Son whom He sent to save the world.

Jesus spent thirty plus years on earth, teaching about Living Water, a New Kingdom, love and hope. Then, another promise was fulfilled in His trial, crucifixion and burial. For three days, God told the heavens and His people to "Wait for it...wait for it...wait for it." Then, Jesus defeated death and rose from the grave which brought another promise to pass.

Now, we live in another time of God's preparation. We struggle through our days on this earth. We face circumstances that seem impossible by worldly standards, but God says, "Wait for it...wait for it...wait for it."

Through Traffic

My brother and his family live somewhat halfway between myself and my parents. One weekend, I had planned to spend some time with my parents in my home town. We met at my brother's, spent the night with them, then got up the next morning to drive to my parent's house. On the way, we took a detour to visit my Mema who lives in a nursing home in yet another town. I did not know the route from my brother's to the nursing home, so I had to follow my parents.

The first leg of our trip was through the Dallas/ Fort Worth area in Monday-morning traffic. And all God's people said, "ewww!" If I did not want to lose my dad's truck in the traffic, I had to follow closely, be attentive and do what he did. If he turned on his blinker, I turned on mine. If he changed lanes, I changed lanes. If he took an exit, I exited too. All the while, contending with merging traffic and traffic on either side. If a car got between me and my parents, I could still see my dad's truck, but if a large truck or semi got between us, I lost sight of my parents. If I wanted to get to where I could see them again, I had get around the vehicle that blocked my view. In order to do that, I had to change lanes and squeeze back in between the larger vehicle and my parent's truck. So, I would turn on my blinker, close my eyes and just go for it. After about an hour and a half to two hours, we finally made it through the metro area and were on open highway. My muscles relaxed a little and the grip I had on my steering wheel loosened. As we got further down the road, I got more comfortable with where I

was and did not pay as close attention. At one point,
I was fiddling with my radio, which unbeknownst to
me, caused me to slow down. I looked back up and saw
that my parents had gotten a little further ahead of
me. So, I had to speed up some to catch back up with
them. I did not necessarily have to follow as closely as
I did in Dallas, but still had to keep them in view so I
could be ready to exit when the time came.

We made it to the small town where my Mema lives.
After we visited with her for a while, we continued our
trek to my parent's house. My mom decided to ride
with me for this leg of the trip. My dad still took the
lead, but now I was not alone. My mom knew the way,
so I did not have to worry as much if my dad got too
far ahead or if a car got between us. Mom could still
get me there.

That trip home reminded me of the journey we travel
as we live on this earth. We are all trying to reach
a destination through this journey. Just as Jesus
called His disciples to follow Him, he has extended
that command to us today. He knows the route. He
knows where traffic is heavy. He even knows where
construction work is being done and how to get around
those detours that we may face. Even more, Jesus
will send someone to ride with us if we need a travel
companion. The decision to follow Him requires us to
follow closely and to be attentive to His moves. There
will be times when obstacles block our view of Him
and we have to make the decision to change lanes and
squeeze back in so we can see Him again.

No matter how you look at it. He is leading. He knows the way home. He has already been there and wants nothing more than for us to join Him.

After a long day, my parents and I finally made it to their house. We were tired. The trip was not easy. We had to stop a few times to stretch and get a snack to help us make it a little further, but we made it. Following Jesus is not always going to be easy. In fact, there will be more difficult times than easy, but the trip will be worth it in the end. Mine was. I enjoyed spending a few days with my parents and got to see old friends as well as some extended family. Hmmmm, sounds a little like Heaven doesn't it? When our journey here is over, those that follow Jesus will join old friends and family members at the *home* He has prepared for us. To top it off, we will be with our Heavenly Father.

So, turn on your blinker, close your eyes and go for it!

My sheep hear My voice, and I know them, and they follow Me; and I give eternal life to them, and they shall never perish; and no one shall snatch them out of My hand. My Father, who has given them to Me, is greater than all; and no one is able to snatch them out of the Father's hand. I and the Father are one.

- John 10:27-30

For this reason you be ready too; for the Son of Man is coming at an hour when you do not think He will.

- Matthew 24:44

The Single Red Leaf

A single red leaf in a crowd of green.
Why is he different?
What does he see?

A single red leaf is not like the others.
Because of a truth
He has discovered.

The truth he knows and tries to share
A New season is coming
So we must prepare.

A promise was made many years ago
Of a Savior's return
God said it was so.

He prepares a place for us to be
With Him forever
For eternity.

The single red leaf tells all his friends
"Jesus is coming!"
"He's coming again!"

A single red leaf in a crowd of green.
Jesus is coming!
Are
      You
           Ready?

Strength for Battle

Ephesians 6 instructs us to put on the full armor of God. That armor consists of a breast plate, a shield, helmet, sword, a belt and even shoes. But have you ever really considered this armor?

In Biblical times, the armor of a soldier would have been extremely heavy and I imagine quite uncomfortable. The breast plate was worn to protect the heart. It would have been made of metal, probably small pieces sewn together like a chain or the scales on a fish. The shields were about 4 feet long and about 2 feet wide...large enough to duck behind but small enough to carry. It was probably made of wood and covered with leather, maybe even iron or metal. A soldier would carry the shield with one arm, so he could fight with the other. Roman soldiers had several types of swords, but they were all usually made of iron or some form of metal. The helmet, of course, was made to protect a soldier's head. It was usually a bronze cast or an iron alloy lined with leather. The helmet not only covered the head, but came down to cover the back and sides of the neck. So, it had to have been fairly heavy and probably quite uncomfortable. The shoes or sandals were made of heavy leather and were usually strapped up the calves to the knee. The bottoms more than likely had spikes or cleats to help the soldier stand firm during combat. Finally, they would "gird their loins." Imagine taking a really long t-shirt and wrapping it around your back, up between your legs and back around again to the back, then tuck all that in a belt. That belt held all the parts of the armor in place and held the soldier's weapons so they would be within reach for battle. If the belt was not secure, the soldier would not be properly prepared for combat.

I don't know about you, but the weight of the armor alone would have taken me to the ground.

A soldier had to be strong. He had to train both physically and mentally for battle.

God provided an armor for His people, where each piece has a significant purpose. However, before a soldier can even put the armor on, he must have the strength to wear it. Ephesians 6:10 says, *before* the armor is even described, "Finally, be strong in the Lord, and in the strength of HIS might." Relying on His might prepares us for the armor, the armor prepares us for the battle. Without His strength, we would not be able to fight.

God has studied the enemy. He knows their strategy. He knows each of His soldiers. He knows what we need before the battle and has provided everything we need during the battle. If we trust in Him, He will bring us to victory.

Now glory be to God who by his mighty power at work within us is able to do far more than we would ever dare to ask or even dream of—infinitely beyond our highest prayers, desires, thoughts, or hopes.

- Ephesians 3:20

Living Bible

The Patience of *Winter*

Winter is a sweet, silly beagle that belongs to a client for whom I have been pet sitting for over 10 years now. Winter has been trained to "sit" and "wait" for you to tell her it is okay to eat. This is incredible for any dog, let alone a beagle. Winter will sit and look at you with those longing eyes until you say, "Go ahead," at which point she will wholeheartedly dig into the bowl of food set before her.

My clients adopted Winter from a local shelter. Once they got her home and acclimated to her surroundings, they began to train her. Her training began with small treats. She learned that the small treats led to something better...that large bowl of yummy food. She discovered the wait was worth it. Eventually, Winter learned the verbal commands led to the same reward, so the treats were no longer necessary. She learned to be patient and that her owner would give her the reward she was waiting for.

The challenge to be patient is never easy. Face it, we hate to wait...for anything.

God honors our patience. We "sit" and "wait" for Him to answer our prayers, to bring healing, to give us direction, or to fulfill a promise. While we wait, we must train ourselves to find Him in little things. This strengthens our endurance. Soon, God gives us the "Go Ahead." At that point, we discover a reward far greater than we could have ever imagined.

My client loves Winter and wants to provide her with the best home possible. Winter began to understand the love her new owners had for her as they trained her. She could have settled for those little treats and gone on her merry way, but she knew those treats led to much more, so she held out for the bowl of food. In the same way, God loves us and wants us to have more than little treats. We could settle for what comes easily, or we can wait for what God has in store for us.

Patience is not easy, but with God, the wait is worth it.

"The Lord is my portion," says my soul, "Therefore I have hope in Him." The Lord is good to those who wait for Him, to the person who seeks Him.

- Lamentations 3:24-25

Piano Ensemble

When I was in first grade, my parents signed me up
for piano lessons. Countless hours of practice, private
lessons, group classes, competitions and tests were a
part of my life until I graduated from high school.
The last several years of my time as a piano student, I
was a member of an ensemble that took part in a state
recital or competition each summer. This ensemble
was made up of 10-12 students from my home town.
The music we played was a duet, so obviously 5-6 of
us would take one part and the other half would take
the other part. We would get up early a few mornings
a week and take over a local music store to practice
before it opened. My teacher always led the ensemble,
even though some students were not under her
tutelage.

The idea of this ensemble was to take 10-12 of us
playing duets on 5-6 pianos and making it sound like
2 people playing a duet on one piano. As we got older,
the duets got more complicated, so we each got our
own piano...therefore, it was 10-12 pianos working
to sound like two. Anyone who has been a part of a
musical ensemble or band knows what I mean by this.
Not only did we have to make sure we were in sync
with the others playing our part, but we had to be
in rhythm with our counterparts. So, it took a lot of
practice, both as individuals and as a group.

Most musical pieces have a section that is more
complicated than the rest - a climax. It would have
been pretty easy for me to let the other students that

had my part "carry me" per se through those difficult parts. I could have just acted like I was playing...the audience would not have really been able to tell one person was not playing her part. After all, that was the whole idea wasn't it? To sound like one piano? I could have just played the easy parts and moved my fingers around to look like I was playing the hard parts then joined back in on the easy parts. But I didn't. I practiced at home in between group rehearsals, and then we practiced as a group. In reality, that part of the song was not just challenging to me but for the others as well. Some students could pick up on the music much faster than others, but for some, like me, it took more work. Nevertheless, we ALL had to practice because we ALL had to get it. We would play the hard parts over and over and over and over...until we got it right and until we could play it by memory. The music became so etched in our minds that we could play it without really even thinking, even the hard part.

Yes, it would have been easy for me to sit out on the tough parts. It really would not have hurt anyone. The music would have continued. The ensemble would have still sounded good, and the audience would not have even noticed. But, I would have missed out. Truth be told, it was always so rewarding to join my fellow pianists in standing before a clapping audience at the end of the big performance knowing how much work we had all put into it, how we had survived the early morning practices, and that we saw it through to the end, together.

God has composed an incredible musical piece. He has appointed us all to play a part. We all have the choice to perform our part or sit back and let the other musicians carry us. In the end, the music will be performed and the audience will applaud. If we do not take part in the music, *we* miss out on the true blessing of taking the final bow with the rest of the ensemble at the end of the big performance.

I know that Thou canst do all things,
And that no purpose of Thine can be thwarted.

- Job 42:2

...who has saved us, and called us with
holy calling, not according to our works,
but according to His own purpose and
grace which was granted us in
Christ Jesus from all eternity,....

- 2 Timothy 1:9

Into the *Deep*

Growing up, my friends and I spent many summer days enjoying a public pool that was within walking distance of our houses. The pool was L- shaped. If I remember correctly, the main part of the pool started at about two feet and sloped to six feet deep. The deep end of the pool curved off from the main part and was eight to ten feet deep. There were two diving boards at the deepest part of the pool. One of the diving boards was your regular/standard board and the other was the high dive, which seemed miles above the ground, but was probably just about ten feet from the ground.

Jumping from the high dive was pretty exciting. Some of my friends could actually *dive* from that diving board, but not me. I could never bring myself to do that for some reason. The thrill for me was to jump from the high dive like a torpedo so I could hit the floor of the pool and kick myself back above the water quickly. I loved to swim, but I was more afraid of the depths of the water than the height of the board.

Recently a friend and I were talking. She had been through a rough couple of years. She made the comment that she did not know how much deeper she could go. Jumping off the high dive came to mind and I thought to myself, "Well, once you hit the bottom, you can use the floor to boost yourself back up above water."

Being under water is scary. When circumstances of life begin to drown you, feelings of being in deep waters can leave you feeling overwhelmed and hopeless.

There is a story in the Bible where one of Jesus' disciples found himself under water and fighting for his life[8]. As he fought the waters, he looked up to see Jesus reaching His hand through the very water that He was *standing* on.

Whether you are about to hit the floor of the pool or you are just barely under water, Jesus can and will reach down to pull you up for air. You just have to keep looking up. And if you do hit bottom, use the floor to your advantage and push yourself up into His outstretched hands.

When you pass through the waters, I
will be with you; And through the rivers,
they will not overflow you. When you
walk through the fire, you will not be
scorched, nor will the flame burn you.
For I am the Lord your God,

- Isaiah 43:2-3a

But seeing the wind, he became afraid,
and beginning to sink, he cried out saying,
"Lord, save me!" And immediately
Jesus stretched out His hand and
took hold of him, and said to him,
"O you of little faith, why did you doubt?"

- Matthew 14:30-31

*T*reelings of Hope

There is a Christmas Tree farm in the city where I live. I have never been there, but have driven by it many times. One January, after the final Christmas carol had been sung, the Christmas decorations were down, and all the stores had cleared out all their Christmas inventory, I happened to drive by the farm. I guess I had never driven by the tree farm after a Holiday season. The scene was gloomy. There were rows of trees, but those rows were spotted with vacant spots where beautiful trees used to stand; stumps were left from trees that had been chopped down to bring Christmas joy to the living rooms of many families. Emptiness best describes what I saw at first, but then I saw the new tree seedlings, or treelings.

The trees that had been chopped down reminded me of the past; those things that have happened and cannot be changed. The treelings suggest what God has in store NOW and moving forward. The small trees were scrawny in comparison to the mature trees around them. They seemed worthless as they were now, but they will grow. Some will grow to be tall, some may have full, thick branches, while others will have branches that reach out further than the others. No matter how they look when they grow to maturity, they will grow to fulfill their purpose; the purpose of bringing delight to a family's living room for some Christmas to come.

Those little treelings reminded of me of a little something I like to call HOPE.

Circumstances may seem gloomy and impossible, but God gives us HOPE. He promises to do something more than we could ever imagine if we just trust in Him.

Look...Observe! Be astonished! Wonder! Because I am doing something in your days – you would not believe if you were told.

- Habakkuk 1:5

These will wage war against the Lamb,
and the Lamb will overcome them,
because He is Lord of lords
and Kings of kings,
and those who are with Him are
the called and chosen and faithful.

- Revelation 17:14

ℳonogram

I worked for a uniform store for over eight years.
We sold medical scrubs, lab coats, and medical
supplies like stethoscopes, blood pressure cuffs and
so forth. About 5 years into my time there, we added
monogramming services to our business. With the
help of these amazing, computerized sewing machines,
we could put names, logos, designs, and monograms
on just about anything. That part of our business
grew and became quite profitable for the company.
We began to monogram for more than people in the
medical field. Towels, backpacks, baseball caps,
children's clothes, pillowcases, Christmas stockings
(so many Christmas stockings)...you name it, we have
probably monogrammed something on it.

I was surprised by the number of people that
brought items in to have their monogram, or initials,
embroidered on them. Not that this was a new concept,
people have been doing that for decades, but I was
still amazed at how much of our business it entailed.
People would have initials stitched on shirts, bags,
pillowcases, handkerchiefs, headbands and even
socks.

When a design, name or monogram is sewn into
a garment or item, it becomes part of that item.
That's the idea; the embroidery is there to stay. A
great concept unless you make a mistake in the
monogramming process. Unfortunately, either by
human error or machine complications, I experienced
more than my share of mistakes while trying to sew

something on an item. Luckily, most of the mistakes could be corrected. All we had to do was take out the incorrect embroidery. Sounds easy enough right? No, this was a tedious and time consuming process. The larger, thicker and more elaborate the design, the harder it was to correct any errors made. But, it could be done. However, no matter how successful we were at pulling the threads out, the outline of the underlying design was almost always left behind; like playing dot-to-dot. Therefore, in order to cover the error, we had to make sure the item was hooped in the exact same spot and that the machine was set just right. It was a very nerve racking ordeal, and sadly, there were times, that despite our efforts to be careful, the item was beyond repair and we had to replace the entire thing and start completely over.

Our initials, or monograms, are important to us. They represent who we are and by having them sewn on an item, we are letting everyone know who that item belongs to.

When we accept Jesus as our Savior, we inherit very special initials, a new monogram. I think we as Christians are too often either embarrassed, too shy, or afraid to show the world who we are in Christ. Or we only allow those initials to show in certain areas of our lives. We are Children of God! That monogram covers every error, or holes left because of our past. It can even take care of those mistakes that are seemingly beyond repair. Those initials should be on everything we own, in bold, bright letters, and we should wear them proudly.

The Spirit Himself bears witness with our spirit that we are children of God, and if children, heirs also, heirs of God and fellow heirs with Christ, if indeed we suffer with Him in order that we may also be glorified with Him.

- Romans 8:16-17

The *Prodigal* Dog

A few years ago, my neighbor called me at work
and told me one of my dogs had gotten out and was
standing in my front yard. Luckily I worked close
to home, so I left work immediately to go take care
of him.

I was a little puzzled by this news. All but one of
my dogs stayed inside when I was away from home.
Kramer, my shepherd mix stayed outside, but he never
got out of the yard. So, while I was driving home, my
mind was reeling with what had happened, who got
out, and so forth.

I turned the corner on to my block and my neighbor
was standing in his front yard. I pulled over and rolled
down my window. He pointed to my front yard and I
just cracked up at the sight.

You see, my pets had gotten accustomed to having
someone home with them all day, so when I went to
work full time after my husband passed away, some of
my male dogs started to have accidents in the house. I
had to figure out how to make this work. So, I bought
some long pieces of fleece that were about a foot wide
and two yards long. I wrapped the fleece around
their waist twice then tied it in a knot on their backs,
creating a belly-band or diaper, per se. Because of the
width of the fleece, the knot on the dog's back was
pretty big. They looked pretty funny, but it worked. On
this particular day, Duffy, another one of my shepherd

mixes, was sporting a bright turquoise fleece with brightly colored dogs printed on it.

Now Duffy is a big, goofy dog anyway, but when you add a colorful diaper and bow, well, he was a sight to see. I can imagine what people were thinking when they drove down the street and saw him. I'm surprised I did not see pictures of him on social media with some funny caption.

I explained the diaper to my neighbor, we had a few more laughs at Duffy's expense and then I took Duffy inside.

Evidently, the wind had blown my front door open. Duffy knew he could open the storm door, so he just helped himself, took a few laps around the neighborhood and then returned home.

A few months before this happened, I was house sitting for someone and my husband was home. He called me real early in the morning to let me know Duffy had gotten out of the house some time during the night. All he knew was he woke up, the front door had blown open and Duffy was gone. He didn't know how long he had been out.

I rushed home from the house where I was staying while my husband and sweet neighbor drove around the neighborhood looking for Duffy. Just before I got home, my husband called me and told me Duffy was home. After he and my neighbor had driven around looking for signs of our dog, my husband told my neighbor to just return home. When they rounded the corner of our block, Duffy was in the driveway looking at my husband as if to say, "Where have you been?"

My dogs have grown past the diaper stage now, and I have had the storm door fixed so Duffy can longer gallivant around the neighborhood at all hours of the night - or day. I love my animals and have done and will do just about anything to keep them safe and happy. While I am sure Duffy enjoyed his excursions around the "hood," probably made a few friends, and no doubt made a few messes along the way, he never lost sight of HOME, and always found his way back.

God has created a loving home like that for me and for you. Sometimes we run out the storm door, terrorizing the neighborhood. You would think we would realize what we have, but we all too often fill the need to do things on our own, or we wonder off into the night. If we keep our sights on HOME, and return there, we will find Him standing on the front porch with arms open wide.

"Return to Me with all your heart...
And rend your heart and
not your garments."
Now return to the Lord your God,
For He is gracious and compassionate,
Slow to anger, abounding
in lovingkindness,
And relenting of evil.

- Joel 2:12-13

For it was fitting that we should have such a high priest, holy, innocent, undefiled, separated from sinners and exalted above the heavens; who does not need daily, like those high priests, to offer up sacrifices, first for His own sins, and then for the sins of the people, because this He did once for all when He offered up Himself.

- Hebrews 7:26-27

And every priest stands daily ministering and offering time after time the same sacrifices, which can never take away sins; but He, having offered one sacrifice for sins for all time, sat down at the right hand of God,

- Hebrews 10:11-12

Collect Call

How many of you have ever made a "collect call?"
Better yet, how many of you even know what a "collect
call" is? This type of telephone call allows someone
to make a call at the recipient's expense. When I
was growing up, cellular phones were not as easily
accessible as they are today. Therefore, I made many
collect calls home when I traveled with friends or my
youth group. I think I even utilized this type of call
when I was in college. Back then – that makes me feel
so old – the calls required an operator to connect the
callers. Today, thanks to modern technology, a human
operator is no longer needed.

In the Old Testament days, the temple was essential to
communication between God and his chosen people,
the Jews. There was a room in the temple that was
called the Holy of Holies. This room was "off limits" to
everyone except the High Priest, and was separated
from the rest of the temple by a long, thick curtain
called the Veil. The Holy of Holies was where God
came to dwell among His people. Once a year, the High
Priest would enter the Holy of Holies to offer sacrifices
and seek forgiveness for the sins of the people.

When Jesus died on the cross, the Veil that secured
the Holy of Holies was torn from top to bottom.
This opened up a line of communication between
God and His People. There was no longer a need to
communicate through the High Priest.

Today, God's people can call on Him, not only for forgiveness, but to give Him praise, discuss a need, make requests, and seek His will. He is available to us 365 days a year, 7 days a week, 24 hours a day – anytime of day, from anywhere. Through the blood of His Son, we no longer need an "operator" and He has already accepted the charges.

*...for the same Lord is Lord of all,
abounding in riches for all who call upon
Him; for "Whoever will call upon the
name of the Lord will be saved."*

- Romans 10:12-13

Webs

One Fall morning, just before dawn, I stood overlooking a client's yard watching their dogs play. As my eyes adjusted to the darkness, I saw a dot the size of a quarter crawling inches away from my face. It was a spider! If I had taken half a step forward, I would have walked right into the spider's web and the spider would have been in my hair, or on my forehead. I made a low pitched vibrato noise as chills raised the hairs on my neck.

Spiders' webs are all too often discovered when it is too late. After all, that is the purpose of the web; to catch its prey off guard before it has a chance to escape.

We often face our own spider webs. Before we know it, our stream of bad choices, little lies, or changes in habits lead us right into webs of addictions, legal issues, health problems, or other seemingly hopeless situations. Then, life drags us in and binds us with sticky threads that leave us feeling defeated, helpless, or afraid.

Spiders weave their webs at night. Satan is like those eight-legged, creepy crawlers. He waits until darkness sets in, then he begins to weave his silky trap. All of a sudden, we find ourselves trapped in his web struggling to break free. However, no matter how bound we become by our sticky traps, we have a Savior. When we simply say His name, *Jesus,* He comes to our rescue and chases away the one that aims to destroy us.

Nothing is ever hopeless when we belong to Jesus. And one day He will come and destroy the enemy once and for all.

Amen!

The thief comes only to steal, and kill, and destroy; I came that they might have life, and might have it abundantly.

- John 10:10

I Stand

Though stripped of all that is within me,
I stand with hands held high to Thee.

Though defeat and failure hold on tight,
I stand with praise to you Most High.

Though I stand alone in doubt and fear,
You cup your hands to catch each tear.

Weak arms struggle to carry on,
Yet your love for me is never gone.

I stand among those that aim to hurt,
Those that do not seek your word.

My hands reach as high as they can,
To you the one who died for man.

No matter what may come my way,
My heart holds on to what you say.

You say you love me and for this you died,
With bloody arms that stretched out wide.

I stand with hands held high to Thee,
To prove to others that I believe.

Until my days on earth are done,
I stand in awe of You...
The Holy One.

yes, with respect to the promise of God, he did not waver in unbelief, but grew strong in faith, giving glory to God.

— Romans 4:20

Splinters

A splinter is a tiny fragment of wood that gets lodged under the skin. Yes, it usually causes a little pain, but it is more of a nuisance than anything. A splinter is so bothersome that we poke and pinch to get the pesky thing out from under our skin, that we only make matters worse.

I wonder how many splinters Jesus dealt with in His lifetime? Do you think He got a splinter while He was lying in the rugged manger His mother laid Him in when He was born? Growing up as a carpenter, I am sure Jesus experienced plenty of splinters in His fingers and hands. I wonder if Jesus felt any splinters when He reached His hand into the basket of fish and bread to feed the 5000? As often as Jesus climbed in and out of a boat, I am sure He pulled a few splinters from His hands and feet. When Jesus reached up to help Zacchaeus down from the tree, do you think one of those pesky things found its way into His hands? I can imagine the pain Jesus felt when the Roman soldiers pushed a *crown* of splinters into His head. And, then there's the old rugged, wooden cross. On one hand, Jesus' body was so battered that He probably could not feel a tiny piece of wood in His back. On the other hand, the very flesh He was born into was ripped from the bone, so the smallest speck could have felt like another lash from the whips with which the Roman Soldiers used to flog Him. A tiny fragment of wood...a simple splinter...Jesus was a man, of flesh and blood (John 1:14[9]); blood that was shed to change the world His Father had sent Him to save (1 John 4:14[10]).

Emmanuel... God with Us.

Jesus as a Baby in a Manger
took on the wounds of the world
and carried them to the cross
where He died as a Man.
But Good News!

That's not the end of the story...

References

1   *Do Love: A Love Hack's Path to Spiritual Maturity* was written by Pastor Andrew Rankin, pastor of my church, Freedom Church. The book was released in 2013. That same year, he preached a year-long series about how we as Christians and as a church should "Do Love" for each other and those around us. I am grateful for a church that loved me and my family through the difficult loss of my husband! I am proud to belong to a church with a heart for missions; abroad, locally, and within.

2   Deuteronomy 6:5 "And you shall love the Lord your God with all your heart and with all your soul and with all your might."

3   1 Chronicles 28:9 "As for you, my son Solomon, know the God of your father, and serve Him with a whole heart and a willing mind; for the Lord searches all hearts, and understands every intent of the thoughts. If you seek Him, He will let you find Him; but if you forsake Him, He will reject you forever."

4   1 Kings 8:61 "Let your heart therefore be wholly devoted to the Lord our God, to walk in His statutes and to keep His commandments, as at this day."

5   Jeremiah 17:10 "I, the Lord, search the heart, I test the mind, even to give to each man according to his ways, according to the results of his deeds."

6   1 Samuel 16:7 "But the Lord said to Samuel, 'Do not look at his appearance or at the height of his stature, because I have rejected him; for God sees not as man sees, for man looks at the outward appearance, but the Lord looks at the heart.'"

7   Psalm 44:21 "Would not God find this out? For He knows the secrets of the heart."

8   Jesus walks on water. Matthew 14:28-33 "And Peter answered Him and said, 'Lord, if it is You, command me to come to You on the water.' And He said, 'Come!' And Peter got out of the boat, and walked on the water and came toward Jesus. But seeing the wind, he became afraid, and beginning to sink, he cried out, saying, 'Lord, save me!' And immediately Jesus stretched out His hand and took hold of him, and said to him, 'O you of little faith, why did you doubt?' And when they got into the boat, the wind stopped. And those who were in the boat worshipped Him saying, 'You are certainly God's Son!'"

9   John 1:14 "And the Word became flesh, and dwelt among us, and we beheld His glory, glory as of the only begotten from the Father, full of grace and truth."

10 1 John 4:14 "And we have beheld and bear witness that the Father sent the Son to be the Savior of the world."

CPSIA information can be obtained
at www.ICGtesting.com
Printed in the USA
LVOW08s0843090317
526598LV00001B/6/P